In Navajo Land

IN
NAVAJO
LAND

by

Laura Adams Armer

Illustrated with photographs
by the Author
and Sidney and Austin Armer

DAVID McKAY COMPANY, Inc.   1962   NEW YORK

In Navajo Land

Copyright © 1962 by Laura Adams Armer

All rights reserved, including the right to reproduce this book, or parts thereof, in any form, except for the inclusion of brief quotations in a review.

MANUFACTURED IN THE UNITED STATES OF AMERICA

VAN REES PRESS • NEW YORK

To

Bertha L. Gunterman

AND

Eugene Conrotto

Contents

1. The Turquoise Trail 15

2. Because I Wore the Turquoise 26

3. A Visit to the Hopi 35

4. Days Spent in Blue Canyon 44

5. Tony the Pony 56

6. When the Thunder and the Snakes Are Asleep . . . 64

7. The Unfinished Ceremony 72

8. I Give You Na Nai 77

9. The Big Snow 84

10. The Morning Star 91

11. Twelve White Plumes 98

Illustrations

CHAPTER ONE

Four generations 17
When winter comes, the thunder and the snakes are asleep . . 20
Ruins in Canyon de Chelly. The House of Dawn and of
    Evening Twilight 23

CHAPTER TWO

His face showed the security of established belief 28
A lake stretched for miles over what had been sagebrush-
    dotted sand 30
Falls of the Little Colorado River 31
The Moon Bearer 32

CHAPTER THREE

Lorenzo Hubbell 36
Typical audience at a Hopi ceremonial 39
You will help the corn to come 40
My camp at the fantastic cliffs of Blue Canyon 42

CHAPTER FOUR

My camp at Blue Canyon 47
Mr. Black Mountain and His Son 51
White-bedaubed clowns—Hopi Delight Makers 54

CHAPTER FIVE

On horseback we start for Betatakin 57
The ruins at Betatakin 59
The small shepherd herds his flock 60
The pony found in Grand Canyon 62

ILLUSTRATIONS

CHAPTER SIX

The young buds rode in wagons with their mothers 66
Hands of the sand painters 68
Making new moccasins for the dance 70

CHAPTER SEVEN

Happily the chiefs will regard you 74

CHAPTER EIGHT

The eighty-year-old courier of the Mountain Chant 78
Inside the House of Song, Na Nai sat with his patient . . . 82

CHAPTER NINE

The Navajos met the cold with calm and fortitude 86
Lorenzo Hubbell in his trading post 88

CHAPTER TEN

Hopi Indian village 92
An old Hopi man, an old kiva, an old belief 96

CHAPTER ELEVEN

My house on the hill 100
Navajo friends at my eight-sided house 103
Moquitso, the Navajo medicine man, who gave me nearly a
   hundred sand paintings now in University of California,
   Berkeley, and Arizona State University, Tucson 104
Laura Adams Armer and Sidney Armer in their garden
   at Fortuna, California 106

About the Author

O N JANUARY 12, 1962, Laura Armer entered her 89th year. She was born in Sacramento, Calif., the youngest of three children. "Nothing turned to gold for father," she recalls, "but we did have food and shelter and books." Her early life in San Francisco centered around an education in art, but the beauty around her was elusive. After six years in art school, she opened a photography studio. "I was successful," she writes. "I photographed celebrities from all over the world—still I was not satisfied with my medium or with what I was trying to express.

"Then one day I received an inspiration—as if a voice had spoken. 'Don't worry,' I found myself saying out loud, 'when you are an old woman you will write what you fail to paint.' So I began life over."

In 1923 Laura Armer made her first visit to Navajo Land. A decade of dedicated work followed. *Waterless Mountain,* written in 1928, was the first fine book to come from her experiences in the Four Corners Country. When it was awarded the Newbery Medal, the prophecy was fulfilled. Mrs. Armer and her artist husband, Sidney, are "spending our last days, surrounded by the groves of beautiful redwoods, in northern California."

In Navajo Land

CHAPTER ONE

The Turquoise Trail

IN THE ARID region of Northern Arizona, the Navajo Indians have lived for centuries. Their environment is dramatic in the extreme. The Grand Canyon of the Colorado River, with its strata showing from the top soil to the bedrock of granite, presents a mile-deep record of the physical history of the earth. Human drama staged amid such stupendous land sculpture naturally is affected by its grandeur. The early Navajos, fighting their way from the north, were overawed by this land in which they found a haven.

Legend tells that at one time they planted crops and lived in stone houses. Today the Navajos are shepherds with small log and dirt hogans for homes. During their wanderings they absorbed some of the culture of the Pueblo people descended from the Cliff Dwellers. Navajo myths are tinged with Pueblo coloring, but always they retain a character of their own. The imagination of these precocious stragglers peopled the abandoned cliff dwellings with supernatural beings. The San Juan River they named the Old Age River, of which they have never ceased to sing:

"That flowing water!
That flowing water!
My mind wanders across it.
That broad water!
That broad water!
My mind wanders across it.
That old age water!
That flowing water!
My mind wanders across it."

Through the years the Navajos roamed the mountains, hunting and gathering seeds, learning to respect the thunder and the rattle-snakes. They made songs as they traveled. These are sung inside the medicine lodge in winter when the thunder and the snakes are asleep. They are part of the healing ceremonies. Medicine men memorize but do not understand these archaic words. They chant and shake their rattles in great earnestness, convinced that the songs of their uncles have power to heal. With the songs, the sand paintings are made. The two are inseparable.

Paintings in dry color on the floor of the medicine lodge illustrate the myths. In them live historic episodes, poetic conceptions and symbolic designs. They are not emotionally conceived expressions of any individual. They are traditional tribal symbols that must not deviate from the prescribed pattern. Only in the decorations of the skirts and tobacco pouches of the gods may the pourer of sand express his personality in patterns of stars, crosses, triangles, feathers or whatever his fancy dictates. The Navajos do not think in aesthetic terms when making a sand painting. Power lies in symbolic verity. The pourers of sand do not doubt that deity is portrayed in manifold phases, nor do the many men, women and children doubt as they come riding from far canyons, some in old wagons drawn by de-crepit horses, many on horseback and a few in wheezing Fords. They come riding to hear the songs, to gossip, to meet old friends and to

Four generations

revel in the stories of ancient times when their forefathers dwelt near the Old Age River.

It was Washington Matthews who first recorded some of the sand paintings and songs of the Navajos in 1885. These were published in an Ethnological Report. In 1887 the American Folklore Society brought out his *Navajo Legends,* a precious volume of understanding of the tribal life of a virile people. He was the first scholar to become aware of the poetry of the Navajos. It is to him that I owe the inspiration that sent me among them; to him and to the Franciscan Fathers of St. Michaels, Arizona, who published *An Ethnologic Dictionary of the Navajo Language.*

I went first as a painter, trying to express the inner longing for the intangible in a land that is cruel and impersonal. As the years passed, I found myself studying folklore and the religious ritual of sand painting. It is necessary to tell how physically difficult it was to enter the Navajo domain. Only through the kindness extended by various white traders was I enabled to work. They helped me in a part of my own country where it was imperative to obtain a permit from the United States government, allowing me to live on an Indian Reservation.

Among the Navajo songs translated by Washington Matthews was one of Dawn Boy telling of a Child of the White Corn wandering in the house of happiness, in the house of long life, with beauty all around him. It was the song of Dawn Boy that decided the route of our vacation in June, 1923. We left Berkeley in a Buick touring car, Sidney and I, our twenty-year-old son Austin, and Paul Louis Faye, a friend who had lived among the Navajos studying their language and customs. We were prepared to camp out in a dry country. The running board of the car held canteens of water and a lunch box. A trunk on the rear stowed a gasoline camp stove with pots and pans. Sleeping bags and ethnological reports filled half of the back seat. Cameras and canned goods reposed at our feet. The baggage was not a complete index of our activities, as paints and brushes were left at home and in my husband's San Francisco studio of commercial art. Luggage all around us, with it we wandered. Austin drove the car, achieving Grand Canyon which we left without taking one snapshot, proving proper restraint and reverence in the presence of majesty.

On a short side trip from the Canyon we met Navajos repairing the road. They were tall men, with long black hair knotted at the backs of their heads. All wore turquoise earrings dangling from pieces of string which went through holes in the ear lobes. The turquoise was cut in triangular form with rounded corners and sides. The blue gems glowing against brown skin spoke of romance of the Southwest, recalling old tales of Spanish conquistadores who, seeking gold, found turquoise; told of Montezuma in regal splendor of turquoise; told of secret desert mines where the life-giving stone awaited the primitive miner. As the song of Dawn Boy had brought yearning to me, so did the turquoise earrings. I asked Mr. Faye if it would be possible to buy a pair of earrings, if so what should I pay?

"If they are heart's desire, pay what equals heart's desire."

The bedecked Indians could speak no English. They were about to return to their camp for the noon meal. We went with them. Their women were roasting mutton ribs, and frying bread in a Dutch oven of sizzling fat. We silently held their proffered hands. We did not shake hands, just clasped. No word was spoken. After a long silence I asked what to do next.

"Offer the price of heart's desire," said Mr. Faye.

I took from my purse a five-dollar bill, held it toward a shy denizen of the desert and pointed to his greenish-blue earrings. From the alacrity with which he removed the pendants and grasped the five dollars, it was evident the price was sufficient. Thus began the turquoise trail which was to lead to the house of happiness among the cliffs.

At Flagstaff, where we were to leave the highway and plunge into *terra incognita,* Mr. Faye gave us explicit directions as to behavior among the Navajos for whom he had conceived a wholesome respect.

When winter comes, the thunder and the snakes are asleep

I was advised not to wear knickers but to don a skirt for the approval
of modest Indians. I complied, adding whatever touch of femininity
I could muster from my suitcase. Filling our canteens with pure
mountain water, we started north. Mile after mile, we rode over a
land without preceived beginning or ending; a land indifferent to
humanity or to anything less magnificent than the sky above. Flat
places lay dazzling in sunshine. Rocks pointed prophetically upward.
Placidly the water holes mirrored the sky, into whose blue merged
the snowy peaks of the western mountains. Dust in the distance indicating a flock of sheep bore a sense of human insignificance. It was
powerfully lonely.

We reached Red Lake Trading Post set upon a rise of ground in the midst of sand. Made of stone and octagonal in shape, the building suggested a frontier fort, especially as the windows were barred with iron. Inside the forbidding walls we met Trader O'Farrell. Groups of Indians, bartering woolen rugs for flour and sugar, leaned leisurely upon high counters. We liked the rugs. We liked the odor of smoke and mutton woven into them along with zigzag patterns of white, black and gray. Barbaric silver jewelry set with turquoise dazzled us by its profusion. We learned that it was pawned wealth to be redeemed by the Indians when money was not needed for soda pop or canned tomatoes. Some of the pieces were for sale. Holding a string of turquoise and white shell in my hands, I forgot that I should be preparing the noon meal. Later, while I opened cans of food outside the store and tried to shelter my cooking from the whirling sand, Mr. Faye presented me with an antique silver bracelet set with one blue stone. I placed it upon my right wrist and continued to stir the soup.

Among juniper-dotted hills we met a woman on horseback. Sure and strong, with calico skirt flapping about her moccasined feet, the desert beauty passed, smiling a welcome to Navajo Land. Austin slowed the car that we might watch the personification of all that was lovely in the midst of austerity. An apple-green plush jacket served as background for masses of turquoise and coral beads. The rider disappeared among the junipers which seemed to bow in obeisance to her beauty.

At the top of Marsh Pass we camped for the night. Distant mesas broke into terraced cliffs whose rocks rose from the banks of a winding river far below us.

It was good to awake to a world of turquoise sky. Every breath of air added zest to existence. Mr. Faye smiled. Austin laughed uproariously at some joke of his father's, a blue jay screamed in appreciation, and the coffee bubbled over. Full of the joy of the morning, down to Wetherill's Post we wandered. It was the Wetherill family that had discovered the ruins of Mesa Verde, in Colorado. We talked of a possible route to the National Park and were told that Mr. Wetherill was driving cross-country in the afternoon to some point in that direction.

No automobile had been over the route he intended to travel!

Next morning we filled the car with gasoline, piled an extra ten-gallon can among the ethnological reports, and followed Mr. Wetherill's trail across the desert.

At Mesa Verde, high in the cliffs, rest ancient rock homes, long since abandoned by the builders. Visitors wonder why human beings sought shelter in a place so difficult of access. Might not the beauty of Mesa Verde with its deep canyons clothed with conifers, with its cliff caves ready-made for shelter, be reason enough for residence there at any time? One accepts the necessity of protection against marauding tribes—the obvious is always accepted. It is the subtle influences that make life worth living to human beings, whether they be stone-age workers or modern machine-age experts. What vast experience speaks in the masonry of the Cliff Palace built by wanderers from the far south! What memories of earnest priests who once sang in the round underground kivas!

After a week of wandering over mesas and up canyons, we approached Canyon de Chelly with its homes of an early people perched high in the rocks. We hired saddle horses at Chin Lee and rode through sand to Red Rock House, the house of happiness of Navajo song. In the silence of midday, with walls of reddish sandstone rising far above the sandy stream bed, we gazed entranced at preliterate man's adaptation of the cliff caves to his domestic needs. The upper story of the dwelling stands painted white. The lower is of yellow-clay color. The Navajos call it the House of Dawn and of Evening Twilight. For them it is the abode of their gods, not to be entered by the people of the earth. It rises in perfect symmetry, hugging the mother cliff high above crumbling ruins at its base. A

Ruins in Canyon de Chelly. The House of Dawn
and of Evening Twilight

pictograph, dimly outlined, lifts its hands upward, some reminiscence of the time when Dawn Boy sang of the beautiful trail.

Reluctantly we left the hallowed spot, carrying with us memories that gave us courage to meet bad places on the way. We encountered a furious dust storm. The wind raged on the bare hilltops. It lifted the sand which once was ocean bottom to whirl it against the sun to darken the earth. Down the washes it rushed with its burden of sand to fling against leaning brush, roots of juniper, gray poles of corrals. Driving became impossible.

We stopped near Leupp Indian Agency to take refuge in Sunrise Trading Post. There we met the trader, Nevy Smith, who regaled us with extravagant yarns, canned sausage, crackers and cheese. Despite certain obesity emphasized by a tightly fitting knit shirt, he possessed sprightliness. Seeing my camera equipment he told us that numerous movie stars and cameramen had worked in his neighborhood but he had never been chosen as a model. He joked so much about his Falstaffian rotundity that I decided to make a study of him to prove that he was as interesting as the rest of the scenery. After we reached Berkeley I developed the plates and sent prints to him. Overcome by emotion, he wrote:

Gentle Lady:
The rubescent party who obstructed the view around the Sunrise Post has received the photographs, the entire four-hundred-dollars' worth. Mrs. Armer, I sure do thank you for your kindness and your thoughtfulness in going to all the trouble and expense, of sending me, an uncouth and half-baked Indian Trader, such photos and so many of them. I am mailing several to the wifie without comment other than "Those Valentino and J. Warren Kerrigan persons were sort of overrated." By the way, I am sending to you the turquoise earrings you liked so much.

The brilliant stones fired me anew to revisit the land where sky-blue gems were found in ancient cliff dwellings. I wished to paint

24

in the spectacular country. The kindly trader helped me to accomplish my desire by offering a room at Sunrise Post, where I could meet Navajos as they came to trade. My husband and son appreciated the offer. They knew the difficulty of finding a lodging on the Navajo Reservation. They could not accompany me. Sidney must stay with his commercial art designing; Austin must continue at college.

CHAPTER TWO

Because I Wore the Turquoise

For my sake bluebird approaches.
For my sake bluebird approaches.
The rain sprinkles.
The corn comes up.
The rain sprinkles.
The rain descends.

T HE RAIN HAD been descending for many weeks, not a gentle rain called by the bluebird. Unprecedented storms throughout the winter had caused the Little Colorado River to flood. Armed with paint, brushes, canvas and cameras, I arrived at Sunrise Post on a rainy day in February, 1924. Bridge approaches were down. A veritable lake stretched for miles over what had been sagebrush-dotted sand. The desert of water was more desolate than the former dry land, what with a few leafless cottonwoods rising gray and death-like out of the lake.

The tales that Navajos brought were sad enough. Snakes and small rodents swimming to high ground infested the hogans. Strong men fighting the water fell ill of pneumonia. Old Mary's young husband

26

worked all night trying to save the sheep which were Mary's. In two days he died of "no lungs."

The trader grew gloomy and gloomier. He no longer told merry tales of adventure. Only Roy, the young interpreter and helper at the Post, kept the courage of a son of pioneers. As the water receded during the week, a gang of Navajos worked on the bridge approaches. Roy watched the work and reported progress. One day when the storm was over and brilliant sunlight shone on the muddy water, Roy saw an automobile drive over the approach which was finished. He knew that the opposite approach across the river was still washed out.

"Stop that car or it will be wrecked!" he shouted to a Navajo workman.

"It is a white man," the Indian replied. "Let the white man die in the muddy water! Let all those white men die!"

Roy warned the driver, then returned to tell me what had happened. I reassured him by insisting that the feeling of enmity was individual. The Indians had been mistreated by unscrupulous whites, but as a whole they responded to decent treatment. We were talking in the store. I was wearing the blue-turquoise earrings. Three Navajos came in to trade. One looked like a "Bad Injun." He scowled when he noticed the turquoise hanging from my ears. Making a motion toward me as if he intended to tear the gems away, he said to Roy:

"The white woman must not wear the blue stones. They are Navajo."

I continued to wear them, feeling their magic. They were as alluring to me as the song of Dawn Boy, wandering in the beauty all about him. They were indispensable there at the Trading Post with muddy water all around. Their blue, more brilliant than a summer sky, helped me to forget the vengeful attitude of the two disgruntled Indians.

In a week's time, the bridges over the Little Colorado River were passable. My host planned a Sunday trip to Winslow to get certain

His face showed the security of established belief

supplies for his housekeeping. I sat down near the fireplace to cogitate upon my attempt to find the "trail of beauty" that had brought me here. In the late afternoon the trader arrived. He was in the best of spirits. The gloom of the last weeks was gone. He added a leaf to the dining table and spread a clean white sheet upon it. He apologized for not having a tablecloth, saying:

"The wifie took all the linen to Los Angeles with her. Now, we're going to have a real dinner. I'm a first-rate salad maker. Just give me a head of lettuce, some olive oil and lemons, a can of lobster, also ditto of petit pois, and I ask no more."

With warm hospitality he brought forth the precious imported articles he had bought in Winslow. He made a salad of these delicacies so difficult to obtain in the wilderness. He opened a can of chicken and even provided a good cake. It was a feast. We ate happily. After dinner we sat by the fireplace and conversed. I went on with my watercolor copies of the designs in the rugs made by the Navajo women. Logs in the fireplace glowed genially. Added to the acrid smell of cottonwood smoke, a strong muttony flavor emanated from a group of four or five Indians conversing with Roy. They were a piratical-looking lot, in varicolored velveteen jackets and turquoise jewelry. One wore a fur hat in the style of an early trapper. Another's black hair was encircled by a red bandana. A third topped his lithe six feet with an added foot of peaked Stetson felt.

The Indians had been lured in from the outer cold, urged by curiosity to see the white woman who possessed picture books of Navajo lore. I had with me Washington Matthews' account of the Mountain Chant which proved an unending source of interest to those neophytes who were studying to become medicine men. There, in undisputed color and exact design, were reproductions of their sacred sand paintings. White magic that, which gave the Indians a sense of psychic security. They felt at home.

When I asked for explanations of the patterns woven into the rugs, an old silversmith, who proved to be a medicine man as well, volunteered to tell what he knew. He said that a certain four-armed figure

A lake stretched for miles over what had been sagebrush-dotted sand

against a white background was Tsisnadzini, the sacred mountain of
the east. Another pattern he called clouds on a summer sky, white
on a gray-blue background. Only a medicine man could interpret
these designs for they were derived from the sacred sand-painting
lore. As the old man waxed enthusisastic over his self-appointed task,
a surly fellow, who had had too evident contact with the whites at
the railroad, announced that the storyteller should be paid because
the curious white woman would make money. Roy silenced him.
He had no influence on the inspired silversmith who answered:

Falls of the Little Colorado River

"Some people do not believe. She believes because she loves the beautiful. She wears the turquoise."

Spontaneously we two clasped hands as artist to artist. I felt that I was nearing the beautiful trail. My happiness was complete. I said to the trader:

"I can never thank you enough for providing this opportunity. It is the contact I needed."

The road to the north was open. It was time to move on toward Oraibi, the Hopi village sixty miles away. In the previous summer I

The Moon Bearer

had noticed scraggly peach trees growing against the bare rocks of Pumpkin Hill. How thrilling they would be when they burst into pink bloom! I must sketch the old trees whose ancestors had come out of Spain with the conquistadores.

Roy's people at a small post north of us invited me to stay with them for a few days. Life at Williams Post kept to an even tenor. Only once did my activities disturb it. I was painting a tired-looking mare, with an end-of-the-trail droop, beside a rickety hogan with desert stretching to distant red mesas. The weather was beastly cold, my fingers numb by the time I entered the store to rest. There, Mr. Williams informed me that the Navajo who owned the pony said that I had cast a spell upon it. The animal was sick.

"It looks to me like a case of bots," he added. "I'm getting a pint of turpentine to pour down its throat. You'd better keep out of sight. If the pony gets worse, the Indian will blame you."

Out of sight I kept, pondering over the accusation of witchcraft. After an hour or two the smiling owner of the bewitched animal entered the room with Mr. Williams. *"Yahtay, yahtay!"* exclaimed the Navajo.

"That means okay. The mare has just foaled. Now, this superstitious native wishes you to paint the offspring. He says you're a good medicine woman, bring him good luck," explained the trader.

The Indian stood looking at the painting, repeating, *"Yahtay, yahtay."* He pointed to the ears of the mare indicating that they were too long and made the pony look like a mule. He clasped my hand as he was about to leave. Gazing at the blue earrings, he said reverently, *"Nezhoni"* . . . beautiful.

The news of a white-haired medicine woman wearing blue-sky stones spread over the country. The Indians were willing to pose in front of the camera. Red Hat wanted me to paint his wife. I wondered if he hoped that the elderly Sarah would produce a Navajo Isaac to be the pride of his old age.

One day there came riding on a winter-coated pony an old medicine man who must have been four-score-ten or more. He was bedecked with turquoise, white shell and coral necklaces. He wore turquoise in his ear lobes. A tobacco pouch hung from a leather strap across his right shoulder, the strap closely set with silver studs. A leather bow-guard on his right wrist indicated that the ancient one had once hunted with bow and arrow. The buckskin moccasins came nearly to his knees and were bound with woven scarlet garters. Altogether he looked like a traveling museum of classic old-time Navajo jewelry.

When asked to sit on the Trading Post steps to be photographed his dignity was great, his pride in his trappings so evident that he rolled his calico pants to the knees to expose the fringed garters. When I stepped close to him to adjust an unruly fold in his jacket,

I was vehemently repulsed. I learned then and there that a Navajo resents being touched. His person is sacred. Just such an old man it must have been in the beginning, who begged to carry the moon across the sky. His face showed the security of established belief. He stood for all the warrior strength of the ancients; all the secret wisdom of a nomad race.

CHAPTER THREE

A Visit to the Hopi

Aᴛ ᴡɪʟʟɪᴀᴍs ᴘᴏsᴛ I had contacted fine types. In two weeks I was ready to leave for the Hopi village of Oraibi. The problem was to secure headquarters in the village. That could only be done through the trader, Lorenzo Hubbell. I had written him that I wished to paint peach trees in bloom. I could get no definite answer as to a roof over my head. The gentleman merely said, "Come."

Roy drove me and my baggage. After many miles through the Painted Desert we glimpsed a village of dull-hued stone crouching upon a mesa top, colorless and insignificant in the landscape, barely distinguishable from the rocks which formed its base. Oraibi, the busy brown people had named it eight hundred years before, when the first stragglers from other mesa settlements founded it upon the barren rocks. Oraibi, it is today, the oldest continously occupied village in the United States. It is a place of buried secrets, underground kivas, and silent little people packing their water from some hole in the rocks, drying their peaches on the messa top, never forgetting the lean years when famine stalked the land.

Lorenzo Hubbell

It was at the modern village at the foot of the mesa, where Lorenzo Hubbell's trading post and the government day school took care of the Hopi population, that I made my home in a one-room stone house, mud-plastered in the interior. Mr. Hubbell had persuaded a Hopi man and his wife to move next door for the price of thirty dollars a month. A good wood stove, a couch, a table and chairs were ample furnishings. Nelly, the Hopi owner, baked delicious bread for me, kept the water buckets filled, brought wood, and was altogether a most helpful and sympathetic friend. But for her I should have been desolate. The conservative Hopis withheld their smiles.

In that little house field mice scampered about at night. I was forced to set traps for them, not a pleasant task. I comforted myself philosophically, knowing that if I were to study primitive life in America, I must take whatever came. I was pondering over that necessity one night as I lay on my cot in the dark. I heard a peculiar scraping sound on the cheesecloth ceiling. I relighted the coal-oil lamp. To my consternation I saw a four-inch centipede wending its way across the cheesecloth. I knew that he must be waylaid. I pulled on my stockings and shoes, covered my hands with paint rags, grabbed a broom and climbed a chair. I brushed the articulated anthropod animal to the floor. With terrifying swiftness, it sought to escape. Discarding the broom, I relied upon the iron rod of my sketching umbrella. I managed to spike the hard-jointed centipede. It was difficult to cut in two. When that was accomplished the parts continued to wriggle and squirm. I had greeted that monster boldly.

The next day, without premeditation, I painted a brown figure with long black hair clasping an olla turned upside down. Not one drop of water fell to the parched earth below. That painting of drouth expressed something of the austere land where elemental powers announce themselves in no uncertain terms; where windstorms spiral the sand, and drouth sears the souls of men with fear.

In the center of the small village of Oraibi rose a sand hill which served the purpose of an arena for the town crier. In the evening, his deep-toned voice filled the air as he stood on the rise of ground, silhouetted against an orange sunset sky. Erect and sure, he spoke to the village people standing near their doorways. Some sat on the ground in front of their stone houses eating their simple meals of beans and corn meal.

They listened with interest to the news. The town crier, announcing a rabbit drive for the morrow, continued in a strong voice:

"Be up before daylight, young men of the village. To the fleetest runners I say: have your rabbit sticks ready. Go to the fields back from the wash. There the rabbits are eating our young corn."

The town crier finished his harangue with one long drawn-out note, which faded into the evening air along with the smoke from the village chimney pots. Then he joined his family group where his three-year-old son played in the sand. The naked golden-brown babe ran to his father who gladly held him on his lap. From his pocket the father brought forth a small dry gourd to which he had fitted a wooden handle.

"This, I have brought for a rattle so that Ete-ee, my little son, may learn to dance to its sound."

The mother of the child laughed the soft laugh of Indian women. Her even white teeth sparkled and her brown eyes showed pride in her baby. "Dance now, for your father, Ete-ee."

The black-haired child lifted one tiny foot and stamped it on the ground in the intricate rhythm learned from his elders. Soberly the family watched the young dancer to see that he made no mistakes.

"You are learning, child," said the father. "You will help the corn to come up and the rain to fall."

The orange light gave way to dusk. The people entered their stone houses. The sky darkened until it became as the black stone of jet, set with sparkling stars brilliant in the desert air. On the mesa tops the Hopi men danced, month after month, long rows of them with white kilts, gay sashes of their own weaving and with elaborate masks over their heads. The audience, sitting against adobe walls and on tops of roofs, included interested Navajos as well as Hopis. Painted bodies of different kachinas artfully represented very old characters in Southwest mythology. I was transported out of the modern world into a fairyland where turquoise-blue and yellow bodies took the parts of birds hopping about the plaza beneath turquoise skies.

In the Oraibi government school the principal, J. Preston Myers, arranged that I teach art to a class of forty Hopi boys and girls. Twenty minutes a day, five days a week, the children quickly dashed off joyous compositions. All I had to do was to point out any occa-

38

Typical audience at a Hopi ceremonial

You will help the corn to come

sional influence of modern magazine illustrations on the schoolroom walls. Mr. Myers, eager to help the children be themselves, copied Hopi pottery designs from ethnological reports and set the girls to embroidering in wool the patterns he drew for them on paper. Inane fancy work, a la ladies journals, was abolished. Corrals, horses, cows, storms, peach trees and mesas took form on paper, with rhythmic beauty of line.

One small boy of seven, who went about the village on crutches because of a tubercular condition of the bones of his legs, haunted my footsteps. He wanted to paint. He had no brushes, no paper, no pigment. I outfitted Waldo Mootska and he went into the sanctuary of a kiva to copy the mask of a Hopi kachina. The result was so astounding that I continued to help him, being more than careful not to influence his style in the least. I marveled at the native ability of the Indian people. I learned more of the real value of design and painting among those people than I ever absorbed in an art school. Later, Waldo developed into one of the fine Hopi watercolorists. One of his earliest paintings shows a Navajo Yay with the tubelike lips which caricature the Navajo manner of pursing the lips and pointing with them.

As August approached, the villagers were absorbed in preparations for the coming snake dance. Mr. Myers had given me an empty schoolroom for a studio. I decided to turn it into a museum of Indian art. Rugs, pottery and jewelry were loaned by the trading post. My canvases hung upon the walls. I longed to have a sand painting of the Navajos on the floor. When I spoke to Mr. Hubbell about it, he said, "You ask for the moon. If anyone can get it for you, I can."

In a day or two he brought to the studio, Ashi, a tall medicine man wearing a faded purple velveteen jacket and much turquoise. Ashi stood in front of my paintings of the myths of his people.

"I will make the sand painting taught me by my uncle," he said to Mr. Hubbell. "The white woman knows good medicine."

In four days Ashi arrived with two helpers. On the floor they spread clean sand from the Oraibi wash. They leveled it with a weaving batten. That done, they proceeded to grind their colors on a metate: gypsum for white of the east, black made of charcoal for the north, the two mixed for gray-blue of the south. Yellow for the west came ready-made from the cliffs. Ashi started to pour the dry colors in intricate designs. Holding the powder between thumb and forefinger, he poured it where his mind willed. From a central square of blue radiated the cloud people in groups of four wearing triangular cloud dresses, one cloud rising out of another. Alternating with them grew the four sacred plants of the Southwest: maize, squash, bean and tobacco. Impressive in design and pastel-like in color, the painting was arched by an anthropomorphic rainbow, red

41

My camp at the fantastic cliffs of Blue **Canyon**

and blue, outlined in white. To complete the work, two strange beings called Dontso were drawn to guard the sand painting, to add their blessing to that of the rainbow.

When the pourer of sand left, I sat alone in the quiet room with shades drawn and door closed. Ashi had requested that precaution. Power of the concentrated authority of tradition emanated from the painting. Every detail was holy, having an esoteric value through the ages. If we could fathom the lore of the Navajos we might compile a history of aboriginal America, so various have been their borrowings.

On that warm day in August as I sat copying the painted Cloud People, a rumble of thunder announced itself in the distance. The voice that beautifies the land was speaking. Again and again it sounded among the dark clouds, coming nearer and nearer, the voice of the thunder. Rain poured down from the clouds. Lightning brightened the room. The windows rattled in their loose frames. I opened the door that I might smell the moistened earth. When the shower passed I walked to the trading post to show the copy of the cloud painting to Mr. Hubbell.

"You asked for the moon and you received the clouds. It looks as if Ashi put one over on the Hopis. Their prayers for rain culminate with the snake dance in four days."

Guests were arriving to witness that ceremony to be held at Hotevilla, the last village on Fourth Mesa. In my schoolroom studio, decorated with green sheaves of corn in native pottery jars, I acted as hostess to those visitors whom Mr. Hubbell and Mr. Myers brought to my door. That was a joy and a privilege, considering the variety of inspired people to be contacted: scholars, painters, writers, seekers of the deep, evasive mysteries hidden in the Southwest.

CHAPTER FOUR

Days Spent in Blue Canyon

Lorenzo hubbell, the trader at Oraibi, often spoke of Blue Canyon as the most beautiful spot in the neighborhood of the Hopi mesas. We visited it one Sunday, driving thirty miles northward from Oraibi, over a very rough road. Past rocky mesas, down to sandy washes we traveled, watching thunderclouds mass above the distant hills. Lightning streaked the purple clouds. Rain fell in torrents, freshening the wild sunflowers blooming in the sand. By the time we reached Blue Canyon, the sun shone on spectacular cliffs rising above the wash where two Navajo families lived with their flocks of sheep. An old hogan of earth-covered logs stood in the sand near a lone cottonwood tree. Convinced that a painter's paradise spread all about, I exclaimed:

"This is where I wish to live! Would it be at all possible?"

"It would be difficult, nothing soft about it, no physical comfort," said Mr. Hubbell. "Are you again asking for the moon?"

"It seems to be the moon itself," I answered, "so desolate is it, so worn and neglected. I feel like giving it life."

Not until the following spring, in 1925, was my camp made at the base of the fantastic cliffs of Blue Canyon. Mr. Hubbell and Herbert, a good Hopi friend, drove me and a truckload of baggage to the remote spot. They set up two tiny tents to hold my canvases, paints and clothes. Near by a cot awaited me when night should fall. My benefactors were about to leave for the trading post. Having said good-by, Mr. Hubbell added a final word as he sat at the wheel of his car.

"If this moon place is not wild enough for you, send word to Oraibi and I will try to find what you want. Be sure to remember the word for water: *toh, toh, toh, toh*. Do not forget it. Also it would be wise to introduce yourself to any strange Navajo as my friend. Say to him, '*Na Kai Tso, bi kis.*' " (Na Kai Tso was Hubbell's Indian name—his friend).

I watched the car turn around, then I moved toward the household goods lying in the sand. With a sense of exhilaration I proceeded to sort them. I arranged things so that Jenny, the Navajo girl who was to cook and interpret, could find the canned goods, the coffee, the eggs and bacon. This last, a precious investment that must be protected from weather and dogs, I placed beneath a turned-down washtub. Two heavy rocks on top of the tub seemed sufficient weight to hold it.

My chores finished, I sat on the cot to survey my domain, to assure myself that I was not dreaming. Lambs called plaintively from the rock corral. Above them loomed vermilion cliffs zoned with white. Below these barren cliffs bereft of verdure, left stark and naked by the ebbing of some long-forgotten sea, my campfire burned upon the sands. Up the wash a band of horses walked slowly toward the water hole.

That first night under the stars I lay on my cot watching the blue-black sky bloom with the incandescence of myriad worlds. At dawn I awakened, marveling at the bird notes which issued from the lone cottonwood tree. A mockingbird announced the joy of the morning in tones so sure and buoyant that I arose full of eagerness to begin my life in an environment which quickened my imagination. Jenny, busy at the campfire, had already made the coffee. Its aroma, added to that of sizzling bacon, hastened my dressing. By seven o'clock I sat sketching at my easel. I worked until the shadows on the cliffs faded away before the mounting sun. In the stillness of the canyon where only a sheepbell tinkled, or yellow beetles buzzed in the cottonwood tree, the austerity of the land challenged me to produce.

The outdoor camp was sufficient so long as the sand stayed in the wash, but when the wind lifted it to whirl in spirals, or to advance in sheets of suffocating dust, I was forced to take shelter in the hogan of my Navajo host. My hair and ears would be full of fine sand, and every wet canvas coated with a film of dust from the desert floor.

Inside the hogan the women spun and wove their wool. There were two sisters in that home. I named one of them the Pretty Lady. Her velveteen blouse, enfolding the straight lines of her back and the curves of her breasts, was fastened at the neck with silver-coin buttons. Silver encircled her wrists. Turquoise and white-shell beads hung on her bosom. A full skirt of figured calico flapped about her moccasined feet as she walked in the sunshine tending to the duties of the camp. Perhaps the kettle of dye needed stirring, or the fire must have another stick.

The small son of the Pretty Lady took care of her sheep, wandering with them as they grazed, and returning in the afternoon to put them in the natural rock corral barred with poles of pinyon. It was he who brought water to my camp. He would come riding a burro loaded with a keg of muddy water. He hung the keg on a juniper tree, and by morning the mud would be settled. He was the least spoiled child imaginable, sweet-tempered, not too shy, perfectly at home in the expanse of sagebrush, sand and rock, eager to accept a cookie or a soda cracker offered in my outdoor camp. I wished to know his name, the name his mother gave him, not to be spoken outside the family circle, and then not in the presence of the child.

My camp at Blue Canyon

One day, while the Pretty Lady, Jenny and I were alone, the name was told to me. It was Hayolkal Ashki—Dawn Boy. The Pretty Lady was a poet. She had not named her child Round Boy, nor Fat Boy, nor Red Boy. He was Dawn Boy, named for the singer of the four songs that give access to the Red Rock House. He was named for Dawn Boy who crossed the Canyon de Chelly on a rainbow, singing as he entered the house of dawn and of evening light:

> *"With the pollen of dawn upon my*
> *trail, there I wander.*
> *With beauty before me, I wander.*
> *With beauty behind me, I wander.*
> *On the trail of the morning, I wander."*

One morning Jenny told me that her aunt was sick. I went to the hogan and found the Pretty Lady brewing herbs on the fire. She had been out before sunrise to gather them while they were still covered with dew. The sister's face was swollen and red. I think she was suffering from erysipelas. For days the sick woman lay in the hogan growing worse and more feverish. A medicine man was procured to sing those songs that propitiate an offended spirit. The Pretty Lady prepared for his coming. Armed with an axe she climbed the cottonwood tree and cut branches of green leaves. She packed them to a summer shelter and piled them conically, making a verdant room. On the floor she placed sheepskins, wood for a fire, pans for cooking. Later she killed and flayed a sheep to roast and boil in the green bough lodge. There, the invalid rested on sheepskins, awaiting the coming of the medicine man.

The Pretty Lady spared no strength to help her sister. By late afternoon everything was ready. The Sun God was nearing earth's end, lighting the red tops of the rocks behind the blue smoke from the lodge. The sheep huddled quietly in the stone corral. Up the wash came the husband with a medicine man. Soon a sound of chanting issued from the green cottonwood lodge. When the singing ceased the Pretty Lady walked out, followed by her sister who was stripped to the waist. Behind them came the medicine man carrying a basket and a bull-roarer. He touched with corn meal the brown back and head of his patient. Then it seemed as if "the whole creation groaned and travailed" as the shaman whirled the bull-roarer in the evening air.

To the sound of the groaning stick, the three figures entered the lodge. Darkness settled over the valley. Jenny came to say good night to me. By the light of the fire I noticed that her face was smeared with charcoal. There was a fanatical gleam in her eyes as she told me that she would listen all night in the house of song while her baby slept beside her. She went back with her child, leaving me alone on my cot.

All through the night sweet juniper smoke carried its message to the sky. Out of the darkness came the sound of the medicine man's voice. By dawn, he sang:

"Hozona hastle,
Hozana hastle,
Hozana hastle,
Hozana hastle,"

meaning that the ceremony was completed in beauty.

While the old man stayed in the camp of the two sisters, he graciously related some of the myths. He told of Estsanatlehi, the Changing Woman. She was the daughter of Dawn Man and Darkness Woman, found on a mountaintop by First Man, and reared by him and his wife. When she became a woman, First Man and his environment failed to satisfy the longings of a daughter of the Dawn. Lonely on the mountain she wandered, knowing nothing of the glory that was to be hers. She was destined to marry the Sun God who built for her a turquoise house on an island in the wide water of the west. Her sons, the twin culture gods of Navajo mythology, traveled on rainbows, destroying the terrible monsters of the earth.

The medicine man said that Estsanatlehi danced on top of the four sacred mountains, wearing costumes of precious gems. On the eastern mountain she wore a dress of white shell.

"Some Navajos call her Yolkai Estsan, the White Shell Woman," he said. "That is not her true name. We cannot speak the true name in the summertime. Only in the medicine lodge when the snakes and the thunder are asleep can the true name of the kind mother be spoken."

In a few days the shaman left Blue Canyon. His patient had improved so that she was able to be moved. The family began preparations to leave the camp by the cottonwood tree, the Pretty Lady having found it necessary to take her sheep to greener pastures. Just a moment of panic claimed me, then I was reassured by Jenny. My host had an obliging brother who lived half a mile up the canyon. He was called Mr. Black Mountain and would welcome me to his retreat.

All of us helped to make the invalid as comfortable as possible. Her blanket and sheepskins were placed in the wagon bed. The sun shone fiercely. Green cottonwood branches were tied to stand upright for shade. My sketching umbrella contributed shade to the woman's face.

The cortege started on its way across the glaring sands. Already the flocks had been herded to the new camp. The Pretty Lady drove the ponies which pulled the wagon. Then came the shepherd boy on his pony. He wore a bright-green felt hat of mine, bought in a San Francisco shop. He had adorned it with a blue-jay's feather. Under his arm rested a pet kitten, on his lap a newborn lamb.

They were gone out of my life, but not out of my mind. Never would I forget the loving kindness of the Pretty Lady toiling for her family. Never could I forget her small son and the wordless understanding between us. Years later the memory of him became a book, *Waterless Mountain,* through which he traveled as chief character.

Jenny and I moved on to Mr. Black Mountain's camp. We found ourselves at the base of tall cliffs where we set up our cots and table

Mr. Black Mountain and His Son

of rough boards her uncle had hauled from I know not where. I continued to paint and to entertain my Navajo friends. I would buy a leg of lamb from them (or was it goat?). Seventy-five cents was the price. Jenny would roast it in the Dutch oven and the whole family would come to eat. Why not? I could not consume a leg of lamb.

One day an Indian rode to camp with my home letters. I was notified that a friend from the University wished to visit Blue Canyon to record Navajo songs. Dr. Lehmer was a mathematics professor at the University of California and a musician as well. He would be accompanied by his son Dick.

When I finished reading the letters, I walked across the wash. I was wearing a much bedaubed painting smock, and must have looked as drab as the country. In the red dust of my outdoor life, I could not keep my white hair white. It had a way of turning pink when I washed it with the precious *toh*. I saw two cars approaching. Mr. Hubbell had driven out as escort to Dr. Lehmer and his son.

The two friends from Berkeley were repelled by the desolate expanse of sand and rock. I have no doubt they expected me to look as spick-and-span as I did at an evening party at home. I realized that a magic wand would be needed to convert the scene into one they would never forget. As soon as Mr. Hubbell left, I began my maneuvers. Jenny opened cans of our choicest food. Mutton ribs were procured to roast over a sagebrush fire. *Toh* was provided and placed behind a jutting cliff where the two men could clean the grime from faces and hands. They returned to my outdoor apartment refreshed and more cheerful. The sun set in surpassing glory, intensifying the scarlet flowers of the gilias, starring the rocks with fire, and turning the silken buds of opuntia to lambent flame. Drabness was forgotten. After our camp supper we talked happily of Berkeley. My keen desire to hear the news from home caused Dr. Lehmer to inquire if I did not feel lonely, staying week after week in the canyon.

"Not in the common sense of the word," I answered. "Any woman who has raised a child or lived with a husband is not lonely in her head. It is too full of the details of their care. She wonders if Tom sent the linen to the laundry or if Dick's socks are holding out, or if Harry is eating the proper food. The trouble is, such details get into the brain and stick. Here with the Navajos I am not hampered by trivialities, but I have learned that one must win his own place in the spiritual world, painfully and alone. There is no other way of salvation. The Promised Land lies on the other side of a wilderness."

Dr. Lehmer's blue eyes gleamed mischievously. "You must be very near to the Promised Land, having experienced all this wilderness. I don't see how you can endure such living conditions."

"I don't see how you can tolerate these long-haired men around," Dick added. "Don't they ever go to a barber?"

I assured him that his discomfort would disappear when he heard the songs. I took time to tell him how important long hair is to the orthodox Navajo; how in the myth of "Dsylyi Neyani", the boy wandering to escape the enemy Utes was aided by the holy ones. In the house of the Butterfly Woman, with rainbows all about, the young wanderer was bathed and his hair made to grow long. Then he was ready to learn the sacred songs. Long hair gives strength, power and beauty. The Butterfly Woman was no Delilah, shearing her Samson.

Soon the Navajo friends joined us. Mr. Black Mountain, sitting on the running board of the car, became acquainted through sign language. By some peculiar instinct he became aware of Dr. Lehmer's interest in numbers. In no time at all he taught him to count in Navajo. The ice was broken. The singing began. Dr. Lehmer succeeded in recording several primitive songs.

After the departure of my guests, painting ceased. I busied myself putting the camp into shape for the arrival of my husband and son. I wanted everything, myself included, to be in fine condition. One morning I awoke feeling quite ill. I asked Mr. Black Mountain to take a note to O'Farrell's Trading Post, fifteen miles away. I expected him to go immediately. As the hours passed I became more feverish waiting for aid. At four o'clock I discovered that he had not left. First, he had walked miles over the desert looking for his horse, then returned to relax in the hogan while his wife killed a sheep and roasted ribs for him. The sun was fast approaching Estsanatlehi's hearth before Mr. O'Farrell arrived with various remedies, oranges and grapefruit. No sooner had he cheered me with his presence than a little Navajo boy came running to camp, calling, *"Jedi, jedi."* This was the name for automobile. Around the cliffs of my recessed apart-

White-bedaubed clowns—Hopi Delight Makers

ment came the Buick from home, with Sidney and Austin bewildered by sand, rocks, and the sight of me on my cot.

We remained two weeks in the canyon, relaxing after months of strenuous activities for all of us. Austin entertained Mr. Black Mountain by soldering wire handles on discarded tin cans, making deluxe drinking cups which our host set in a row on the sand for the edification of his family. The mores of the Blue Canyon dwellers had taken a sudden flight into civilization. Mr. Black Mountain craved more and more cups with handles. Austin was obliged to call a halt in the manufacture as he was using tinner's soft solder taken on the trip for mending gasoline leaks on the Buick. He watched Mr. Black Mountain polish silver buttons he had made by pounding dimes into conical molds. Austin saw a chance for more fun. He produced a can of Bennet's Brilliantshine and helped in the polishing.

"*Yahtay, yahtay!*" exclaimed the Navajo, gazing in admiration at the shining buttons all ready for his new velveteen jacket. Everything was *yahtay* for us there in Blue Canyon. We took short side trips, going once to Oraibi via Hotevilla where we were fortunate enough to witness a Hopi ceremony. Old and young were taking part. The women, busy with their piki making, mixed their corn meal with juniper ashes and water, spread the batter on hot rocks to cook and skillfully rolled the blue-tinged paper-thin bread to pile in heaps for all of the villagers to feed upon. When the dance began, a group of white-bedaubed clowns was much in evidence. Undoubtedly they were counterparts of the ancient Delight Makers of whom Bandelier wrote so graphically. Their antics pleased the Hopi onlookers sitting on the village roofs, nearly every woman provided with an up-to-date umbrella.

CHAPTER FIVE

Tony the Pony

WHEN WE LEFT Blue Canyon, traveling to Kayenta, we decided to visit the cliff dwellings of Betatakin. Horses for us and a guide with a pack animal were procured at the Wetherill Post. The trip up a canyon of red rocks was glorious. The guide chose our camp for the night and took care of the horses while we prepared the supper. I wondered what hurt he had suffered in the past, for he seemed so reserved. We opened a can of peaches for dessert and passed some to him. His acceptance answered my pondering.

"Thank you, folks. I sure do like peaches. That last party I took to Rainbow Bridge liked them too, most as much as he liked himself. He ate them all without so much as giving me a sniff."

"Why was that?"

"Must have been a habit learned in a city. Out in this country when a man thinks of number one every minute things usually happen to let him know there are other inhabitants around. For instance, there was that rubber mattress of his. It had to be pumped full of air every

On horseback we start for Betatakin

night. He couldn't sleep on the ground. I had to pump it at night and pack it on the mule in the morning. It was sort of natural toward the end of the trip to stow the rubber contraption so it would get a puncture."

The young guide joined us at the fire, all shyness gone as he repeated, "I sure do like peaches." We opened another can. When twilight came as a soft blanket to enfold us, the guide told stories of remote cliff dwellings in Utah, in some green, watered valley which must have been Eden, so alluring did he make it. He told of old pottery, remains of baskets, the usual mummy or two, but he said what he liked best in that watered valley were the wild ponies. He proceeded to tell us a yarn which is of no archeological value. It was too weird a tale to take seriously, but it fitted the eerie atmosphere of the cliff-dwelling country which for thousands of years had known the struggle of man's mind and body to come close to the powers of nature in his great need to survive and to know that "Which is, and which was, and which is to come." The guide continued:

"You know I'm a born horse wrangler. I had my ropes and I started out at sunrise one morning to look for wild ponies. I was riding Tony, the toughest little pony for getting over rough places. Now Tony, with no lead from me, frisks straight up a mountain with the sun in our faces. He was quivering to beat the band. Once in a while he whinnied, excited-like. I gave him the reins and he landed on top of a ledge where grew a bunch of aspens. The leaves were not shaking, but there seemed to be something alive in the trees. Maybe it was only the light shining through them, but that Tony, he saw something else. He went tearing along between the scattered aspens, with the sun still in our faces. Believe it or not Tony and I found ourselves viewing ten small white ponies pawing the ground in a circle near a dark pool of water. I made Tony stand still. He was trembling. It was enough to make a man feel queer, let alone a horse."

The guide looked wistful and disturbed as he continued:

"The queer thing is about me, a born horse wrangler. I never thought of roping those white beauties. They were undersized animals, who acted different from any breed I knew. They pawed the ground on the east side of the pool, then on the south, then west, then north. I couldn't help thinking about the Fire Dance in the corral when the Navajos, all painted white, move around the fire in the same direction. While I was thinking about those spooky Fire Dancers, I heard an owl hoot. The ponies vanished. By that time the sun was no longer in my eyes. I got off Tony and walked to the

The ruins at Betatakin

The small shepherd herds his flock

pool. There wasn't a hoof mark in sight. Tony followed after me, nibbling at grass. He seemed as much at home in this green place as you and I do on Thanksgiving Day when we eat turkey with the old folks. It seemed that he was extra happy on that high mesa."

My son asked if there were any cliff dwellings in the neighborhood, and was told there was a cave facing south, not a very big one, with ruins of a small village in it, with plenty of broken pottery, coiled ware and some fine pieces of black on white. The storyteller resumed his yarn.

"While I was poking around in the rubbish at the back of the cave I came across some fossil bones. They were horse bones, but so small I couldn't believe my eyes. When I found a skull it wasn't much bigger than a coyote's head. The jaws showed where there had been forty-two teeth just the same as Tony has. If you have any dealings with horses you look in the mouth. Here I was finding a fossil horse in an old cliff dwelling. That's strange, too, because today Indians don't associate with bones. The Navajos call them *chinde*. That means ghost in their language. What I liked best up there on the mountain was the way I felt about Tony. I knew he was back where his ancestors came from. He knew it, too. He had that feeling of belonging to a place."

The guide looked wistfully into the dying embers of the campfire. He sighed and said, "Sometimes I wish I was a horse."

He moved off into the dark. We lay down in our bedrolls, quite content to be together in the great wilderness. In the morning we saw Betatakin. That is a Navajo name meaning Hillside House. On our horses we approached a reddish sandstone cliff made all the redder by the complementary green of the woods at its base. A shadowed cave in the cliff yawned wide, roofed by the overhanging ledge. The trail to Hillside House left the woods to wind around the foot of a tallus slope dotted with pinyons. Just as we climbed to the floor level, our guide, who overnight had become the official statistician and exponent of material facts, pointed to a spring coming out of the rock. Above it, a pictograph showed a human figure with upraised arms on each side of which was a curved line. Next to this personage some kind of horned animal had been painted. The guide said:

"It can't be a mountain sheep because the horns are not spiraled. Maybe it's an antelope. Now let us view the old houses. The cave is four hundred and fifty feet long and two hundred and fifty deep."

Hillside House was my idea of a homesite. Here were what could have been advertised in cliff-dwelling days as modern improvements: running water, solar heating, shade and shelter made by a beautifully colored sandstone roof. My desire for a house in the wilderness increased as I pictured the possibility of working quietly, painting murals in my private apartment, weaving perhaps, and studying trees and flowers of the magic land.

The pony found in Grand Canyon

I was brought back from the flight of fancy by the guide's remark that we must return to Kayenta. We said good-by to Hillside House and rode back down the canyon. The spell of the country stayed with me. When the guide told the legend of a spring in the neighborhood which occasionally gushed forth, showering the rocks with carved turquoise, I felt that my mind could absorb no more. I knew that the desert had claimed me for all time. There was no turning back on the turquoise trail. I played with the thought that man's unconscious mind goes back to the time when he was brother to the animals, understanding them, loving them at the same time that he ate certain of them for food. I knew that I had touched early animistic belief. I knew that our guide to Betatakin could not help but feel its influence. To him, Tony the pony had as much right to a soul as himself. In a desert land, living is so difficult, providing of food so constant an occupation, that man needs recreation. He finds it in fancy, in the making of ephemeral sand paintings on the floor of the medicine lodge, and the dancing of Katchinas in the pueblo plazas.

It was years later, when my husband and I had moved to the redwood country of northern California, that a photographer came to our little town. He had been in the Grand Canyon at the time certain very small ponies were found there. He photographed the finder and the ponies on the north bank of the canyon. Generously, he gave me the negatives and prints he had made. To be sure, the ponies were not white, but they were so small the finder could hold one in his arms. In that great Southwest, I agreed that there was no use asking questions.

CHAPTER SIX

When the Thunder
and the Snakes Are Asleep

THE BACK-TO-BACK month was with us, the time
when winter and summer meet; the new year to go on and the old
to retrace its steps. It is not the lonesome October of the poets. The
skies are not ashen and sober. The leaves are not crisp and sere.
Pinyons are as green as ever in the back-to-back month. Junipers
bear numberless blue berries which drop to the ground, forming
halos about the brown trunks of the trees. The blue halos chime
with the color of the mountains. October is the time of no clouds in
the sky, of no winds on the mesas, the time when the blue smoke
from the hogans lifts straight up to the turquoise sky.

Festivity was in the air in this autumn of 1927. The Night Chant,
a nine-day healing ceremony of the Navajos, was to be given at Pinyon. George Hubbell, with his wife, was in charge of the store,
having taken Henry's place. They made me comfortably at home.
Working and studying conditions were perfect. Frank Walker, part
Navajo, was to be my interpreter. With quantities of sand-colored

paper, jars of poster colors and loads of photographic material, I was prepared for intensive activity. Permission to record the ceremony must be granted by the medicine man and his patient.

Hubbell held a long powwow with the two, who argued, "Why should we allow the white woman to see ceremonies which our own women do not see?"

When that objection was brought to me, I answered, "Tell them not to think of me as a woman, but as an artist."

How Hubbell managed so subtle an argument, I do not know. Only one of his understanding and sensitivity could have done so.

A message came back, "Let the white woman come because she wears the turquoise."

The Indians requested that I wear the earrings always. They said that life-giving powers are spoken of as turquoise blue. They tell of the Turquoise Horse who travels a turquoise trail in the deep above. In summertime his hoofs are shod with silver. He treads upon the far side of the clouds. Is that why every cloud has a silver lining? The mane of the Turquoise Horse is strung with white-shell beads. His tail is a comet of silver strands swishing the pale star-flies away. You can feel his rhythm as he moves among the pillars of the sky.

The heavenly blue sent a benediction to all of us there on the desert sands. Men, women and children came from faraway hogans to hear the songs of their fathers, to watch the dancers of the ninth night, and to renew their faith in tribal gods. The landscape blossomed with wagons covered and uncovered; with women wrapped in gayly colored Pendleton robes. The young buds rode in wagons with their mothers, mostly a joyous lot out for a holiday beneath a turquoise sky. The arid land seemed to exult in what it had produced. Small herds of sheep huddled near bales of hay brought for the stock. Provision was made for man and beast. Mutton was provided and plenty of bubble-bread browned in the iron pots.

The medicine lodge stood completed, made of clean pinyon logs, hand-hewn. A blanket covered the entrance which opened to the east. Many young horsemen, wearing their felt hats, lined up to the

The young buds rode in wagons with their mothers

north of the lodge to survey the proceedings. They were a colorful lot, all wearing turquoise earrings. Most of them had long hair knotted at the back of the head and wound with cotton strings. The hairdo was perfection itself when a good-looking young man like Mose brushes his black locks carefully after washing them in yucca suds. The orange-silk handkerchief about his neck was most becoming to his brown skin. Obligingly Mose removed his big Stetson sombrero and allowed me to photograph his profile.

On the third morning the patient indulged in an outdoor sweatbath. A trench had been heated with hot rocks and filled with aromatic herbs and boughs, upon which the patient was to repose.

Hasteyalti and Hastehogan attended him. On the fourth day, I was invited to witness the purification ceremony. Frank Walker, lifting the blanket from the doorway, directed me to walk sunwise around a small fire in the center of the lodge. He and I sat at the northeast end of a circle of forty Navajo men. We sat upon sheepskins placed upon the sandy floor.

The faces of the old men were kind. Sorrow, hope and resignation were written upon them. No meanness nor cruelty showed. The medicine man and his patient sat on the west side. All was quiet. Opposite me the first man in the circle held a small buckskin bag of pollen. He took a pinch of the powder between thumb and forefinger, touched his lips and the top of his head with the powder, and then tossed the rest toward the sky hole. He passed the bag to the next man. I watched carefully as it went its rounds, so that I should know what to do when it reached me.

All eyes were fastened upon me as I applied the sacred powder to lips and head and offered it to the sky. Feeling that I had passed the test, I was taken aback when Frank Walker whispered, "For what did you pray? They want to know for what you prayed."

I had not known that I was to pray. I said calmly, "I prayed for good weather for the ceremony."

Their faces showed that my words were acceptable. The medicine man began to chant and to shake his gourd rattle while the patient removed his clothing, piece by piece, handed each article to an assistant who dipped them in a basket of yucca suds. Even the turquoise necklace was purified, and then the string which held the queue of black hair. The hair itself was dipped in the suds. A ray of sunlight fell upon the patient's bronze shoulders as he leaned over the basket. After the bath, the assistant rubbed corn meal over the skin and the man redressed.

The next day the first sand painting was made on the floor of the lodge. I sat with my paper and water colors, ready to copy the intricate patterns as ten young men poured the sand held between thumb

Hands of the sand painters

and forefinger. The clean sand which was spread on the floor was smoothed with a batten stick. The painting was begun in the center so that the men could work out from it. They kneeled on the floor as they worked. In the middle, a blue circle indicated water surrounded by a line of white foam, yellow pollen and blue-and-red rainbow. From the pool, black lines representing spruce logs reached from west to east and from north to south, forming the cross of the four quarters. Between them, springing from the pool, grew white roots of four domestic plants, three roots for every plant. The maize, the tobacco and bean were painted blue. The squash vine was black, bearing four squashes of the four cardinal colors. Beautiful birds were drawn on top of the plants.

Figures of the holy ones with their wives were made to stand on the whirling logs. The pattern took on the form of a swastika. Now that the holy ones were embarked on their whirling logs to spin happily about the lake, I could imagine them singing their good songs of the arrival of maize, the planting and the harvesting. All was ready for the portrayal of the four gods who stood at the cardinal points. Three of them were drawn with ornamented canes with which to guide the logs as they whirled. The fourth, standing as guardian of the east, was the white Hasteyalti, the Talking God, with a blue squirrel dangling from a red-and-blue string.

When I started to copy the squirrel, all the young men stopped their work to watch me. One said, "She cannot draw a squirrel."

That put me on my mettle. I took pains to copy exactly. After that test I was accepted by my fellow artists. It was a sort of squirrel initiation. When the painting was finished the patient sat on the west side of it, facing the east. Sacred corn meal was applied to his body, incense burned at his feet. The ceremony consisted of endless details, every one important for restoration of health.

For three consecutive days paintings were made. Many details of paintings and of songs have to do with the culture of the corn which is the main subsistence of life of the American Indian. On the day when the third painting was made, boys and girls were initiated outside of the lodge. They sat in a semicircle on the desert sand. The boys were stripped to the loin cloth, the girls dressed in their very best. Some mothers and grandparents sat near the girls. All heads were bowed, for the uninitiated must not see nor know about the masked gods called yays.

The trusting boys and girls sat on the ground as their ancestors had done throughout the centuries, not knowing what mystery was to be enacted by the yay with a yucca whip. Crosses of corn meal were drawn on the chest of a naked boy who stood upon a blanket. One yay struck him twice with the yucca leaves. The blows were gentle, causing no pain. An ear of corn with short spruce boughs was applied to the feet, the palms of hands, back, shoulders and heads of the girls. After this the representatives of the yays removed their

Making new moccasins for the dance

masks. The children were supposed to be surprised, but no change of expression showed on their faces. They accepted whatever came their way, unquestioning and in faith. They were a serious group of young people, learning something of the great need of human beings to keep in touch with Mother Nature, to know the ways of growing corn, beans and squash. After initiation they could look upon the marvelous sand paintings and learn to pour the sand themselves in patterns of beauty, symmetry and symbolic verity.

Thus are artists made among the Navajos, artists who feel the rhythm of the universe and the wonder of all things animate or inanimate. They learn to sing when the Morning Star arises at dawn, "Big Star, I am your child. Give me the light of your mind that my mind may be light."

The masks used at the Night Chant had a most romantic history. They were owned by a medicine man who was the uncle of the shaman who presided at the ceremony I witnessed at Pinyon. Very old, handed down from uncle to nephew through many generations, they were hidden in a cave in Canyon de Chelly at the time of the Navajo exile to Fort Sumner in 1862. Years later the medicine man and his nephew returned for the precious deerskin masks. They were repainted for every ceremony and finally came into the possession of the nephew. When I showed him the Ethnological Report containing James Stevenson's account of the Night Chant with reproductions of sand paintings and masks used at Keam's Canyon in October, 1885, the shaman-nephew was moved almost to tears.

He said to Hubbell, "It was my uncle who gave the ceremony forty-two years ago. I helped him at that time."

I allowed the tears to blur my eyes. Being blurred, they saw as in a mirage the generations of priest-poets pouring colored sands in patterns of hope as they chanted the songs of the House of Dawn and of Evening Twilight. I did not remain for the ceremonies of the ninth night. I felt that I could absorb no more. There was much to think about.

I sent the films home to be developed, and worked for a few days in Oraibi with Ashi, who wished to give me more sand paintings. We sat on the floor of my room, painting cactus people and the four winds. Ashi seemed impressed by my ability to work, so much so that he named me the Hard-working Woman. I liked the name. It was neither flowery nor false. The Hard-working Woman had little time for frivolity. Its nearest approach came on Thanksgiving Day when Hubbell asked me to witness the doings of the ninth night of another Yeibichai Dance.

CHAPTER SEVEN

The Unfinished Ceremony

W E STARTED FROM Oraibi on Thanksgiving Eve, 1927, driving via Blue Canyon. Lorenzo Hubbell, Jr., was in the best of spirits, singing snatches of Navajo songs as we rode, and smoking a fragrant cigar between songs. We reached my old campground at sunset. The weather was superb, rocks glowing, everybody happy. At the new tent trading post we stopped for hot tomato soup. We made room in the car for an old Navajo who favored us with a traveling song. At dusk we encountered a Ford holding seven young men, not one of whom could make the car go. Mr. Hubbell blithely took it in tow as far as Cow Springs where we learned that we were a day too early for the ceremony. The jovial keeper of the post at that place joined his wife in urging us to stay with them overnight.

There was much of interest in the store. Aside from the usual rows of canned goods, bolts of cotton cloth, soda pop and notions, one shelf held treasures produced in the land—a miniature Aladdin's cave. Out of an ancient pottery bowl, the trader poured a collection of red garnets. He called them rubies. Casually he said:

"The red ants bring these gems out of the ground. The Indians find them on the large anthills some miles from here. Would you like to have these two?"

I accepted the stones gladly. My attention was centered on a large olla decorated with an intricate pattern in white and black. It was a prehistoric piece of pottery found in the neighborhood, representing the best period of designing of the ancient people. It brought visions of a black-haired woman carefully polishing her jar and drawing firmly with a yucca-leaf brush the pattern which flowed out of her mind, a cloud pattern created centuries before by her ancestors who used this magic to bring the rain.

Mr. Hubbell knew what the pottery meant to me. He suggested that we hunt for a piece on the site of the old pueblo near by. We walked over the sand toward a large pond. White Mesa rose in the distance. The ground was littered with sherds, but we found no unbroken pots. Walking in the clear air of that Thanksgiving Day, I spied at my feet a piece of turquoise the size of a thumbnail. It was bluer than any I had ever seen, bluer than the precious gems I wore in my ears.

"Well, what do you think of that?" exclaimed my companion. "I never went walking with anyone who could pick up turquoise on the trail."

What a glorious Thanksgiving Day that was! When evening came we parked the car behind Navajos at the dance site. The weather was freezing cold. Mr. Hubbell wrapped the car radiator in a blanket before we walked a short distance to the scene of action. Hundreds of Navajo men, women and children were huddled about campfires which lined the sacred avenue leading from the medicine lodge to the green room where the dancers were donning their costumes. The crowd was prepared to stay until dawn.

Back of the fires was piled a barrier of saddles, blankets, sheepskins, cooking utensils and mutton. Brilliantly colored Pendleton robes caught the flare from the fires. Turquoise and silver necklaces, earrings, bracelets and rings vied with silver-coin buttons on velveteen

Happily the chiefs will regard you

jackets. Fur caps protected the ears of many of the men, but mostly the tall Stetson was in evidence. The audience awaited the coming of the dramatists whose stage was the avenue in front of the medicine lodge.

The Indians' ability to wait patiently and to enjoy what to us seems tiresome repetition is one of the characteristics to be acquired before one can enter thoroughly into the spirit of their lives. As I waited, thinking of how many times these Indians had been to identical affairs, I was reminded of certain white people who read Dickens' *Christmas Carol* every Christmas Eve, and also I thought of our fathers who never missed a performance of *Hamlet*.

Here was the same interest. The words of the songs, the actions of the dancers must be correct, orthodox and classic; and being such

74

could not fail to get response from a people whose tradition is rich and inspiring.

At that particular ceremony the patient was a woman. She came out of the lodge accompanied by a clansman. They stood on sheepskins facing the east. The shaman advanced toward the patient followed by five mythological characters. Hasteyelte, the Talking God, led the first four dancers who were impersonating corn, rain, vegetation and corn pollen. These four were partly nude, painted white, wearing silver belts and kilts with foxskins hanging from the waist. Slowly, in single file, they advanced toward the patient. She moved quietly down the line of whitened, firelit bodies, scattering the sacred corn meal on them. She repeated in a low voice the invocation the shaman had taught her:

> *"You who dwell in the house of dawn*
> *In the house made of the evening twilight*
> *Where the dark mist curtains the doorway*
> *The path to which is on the rainbow*
> *Where the zigzag lightning stands high on top,*
> *Where the he-rain stands high on top*
> *Oh, male divinity! Come to us, come.*
> *Come with wings which are hung with rainbows . . .*
> *. . . I have made the right offering;*
> *Prepared for you a smoke.*
> *I have asked that the roots of the corn be watered.*
> *Make well my feet, my limbs, my body.*
> *Restore my mind; restore my voice;*
> *Today remove your spell from me."*

After the prayer, the first four dancers returned to the green room and twelve dancers came into the firelight. They held spruce twigs and gourd rattles in their hands, as they had been represented in the sand paintings. Their song was slow at first, but as they proceeded, lifting their right feet in unison and balancing on their left, a fervor grew upon them. Three times they had thrilled the crowd and were expected to appear again, when an unusual quiet settled upon the audience.

"Why are they so still?" I asked.

"They are always quiet at a Yebichai Dance," Mr. Hubbell answered.

"But they are extremely quiet. I feel that something is wrong."

Then an old Navajo whispered, "They say the women are crying."

It was very cold. Wrapped in my blankets I had drawn close to a fire where the kind people had brewed me some tea. I offered it to my Navajo neighbors. It was refused. I knew that tragedy was in our midst.

The old man spoke again. "They say her child is dead."

Not another word was uttered. The dancers did not appear again. The small son of the patient had died in his father's arms a few feet away from where we were preparing to feast on mutton and corn tortillas. The nine days' sing with all the hopes for health, with all the terrific effort of nightly chanting and daily ceremonies, with all the expense of sheep and flour to feed the multitude was now of no avail. He who lives in the House of Dawn where the dark mist curtains the doorway had not heard the prayer of the mother, or having heard had meted out the fate that is so difficult for mere mortals to understand.

CHAPTER EIGHT

I Give You Na Nai

THE YEAR was 1928. Lorenzo Hubbell, Jr., was much interested in the photographs I had made at the ceremonial at Pinyon the previous autumn. He suggested that I direct a motion picture of the Mountain Chant.

In the following weeks I studied intensively the description of the ceremony as witnessed by Washington Matthews. On the margins of his Ethnological Report I made notes as to where the two cameras would have to be positioned. There could be no rehearsing of the ceremony which was to be given near Ganado.

I was taken to this settlement to meet the Hubbell family who lived in the historic adobe built by Lorenzo Hubbell, Sr. On arriving, I learned that the medicine man who was scheduled to conduct the ceremony had become ill. Another singer must be found. The patient, Hasteen Tsosi, had been dreaming of bears and of his child who had died some years before. He needed help.

Mention was made of a certain Na Nai whose knowledge was great, but who was physically imperfect. He had been born without

The eighty-year-old courier of the Mountain Chant

of Klishtso, the great serpent who carries the stars upon his back. The fire symbolized the North Star. The night was stormy and threatening. The silence of two thousand Navajo onlookers waiting for old Na Nai proved that his fear of ridicule was baseless, when he had said, "The people will only see Na Nai, the singer without feet."

The silence enfolding the Navajos made them one. The great fire leaped to black depths above as Na Nai came through the eastern opening of the dark circle of branches, a little gray figure with white hair, oblivious of physical defects, thinking only of the holy office he must fulfill to complete the healing of Hasteen Tsosi. The silence of two thousand tribesmen transcended any ovation a white audience could give to a beloved performer. Here was the power of sincerity, of simplicity and of faith.

After various entertainments prepared for the evening show came the fire dance, the spectacular event of the nine-day ceremony. The tall trees piled conically in the center of the dark circle had been burning fiercely all evening. The fire light shone on the assembled tribesmen awaiting the coming of the fire dancers.

Out of the east they came, ten nude young men, their bodies painted white. In their hands they bore bundles of shredded juniper bark. They halted east of the fire—their sculptured bodies gleaming white in the light. They formed a line facing the fire, waving their bark toward it, taking mincing steps back and forth. Four times they moved sunwise around the blaze, dancing in the four directions. The leader lighted a faggot at the fire and touched it to the shredded bark. Wildly the white figures ran about the roaring flames. The torches grew brighter and brighter. At times the burning brands were applied to the backs of those in front. Dancers threw themselves upon the ground wriggling as close to the fire as possible to relight their extinguished torches, daring with their naked bodies to do obeisance to the Star of the North, daring to greet the winds of the four quarters, daring to meet Cold Woman and her flock of snowbirds.

Inside the House of Song, Na Nai sat with his patient

Toward the end of the festivities came the bear dance. It was not spectacular, but extremely significant in indicating that the ancestors of the Navajos had brought with them from the Far North a memory of bear festivals. The impersonator of the bear crawled on all fours. He was clad in bearskins, and was led by a man with a rattle. Twice he lumbered around the fire, occasionally lunging toward the spectators. Before the long night's ritual was finished, snow fell from the clouds. When dawn came, a white world stretched for miles—pure, serene, a promise of good to come from the earth. While the people packed their pots and pans to carry home, the small company of chanters in the west sang:

"The curtain of daybreak is hanging,
from the land of day it is hanging."

Inside the House of Song, Na Nai sat with his patient. He blessed him with pollen that he might go on his way assured of health, good dreams and peace. With closed eyes, impassive, calm and content, the gray-haired shaman chanted, his lips barely moving. As he proceeded he lost consciousness of his surroundings. Far spread the bright land of his dreams. The trail of his mind led him back to the Old Age River, that flowing water where dwell the beneficent gods of his people.

CHAPTER NINE

The Big Snow

I N THE WINTER of 1931 I lived in a furnished apartment in Winslow, Arizona, busy writing my second book, *Dark Circle of Branches*. John Curly, a young Navajo, was engaged as interpreter. He called me shama, which is mother in his language. I was writing the story of an old medicine man who was born without feet. He was called Na Nai, he who creeps. John Curly proved untiring in ferreting out the facts of Na Nai's childhood. More than once Lorenzo Hubbell, Jr., drove us across the snow-splotched desert to the old man's hogan.

The winter weather came early. Snow fell in flakes until land from mountain peak to sandy wash was buried beneath a wintry blanket. Cold Woman blocked the trails of the wood choppers. Hungry sheep huddled about the hogans. The soft snow would not hold their weight. Navajos shoveled snow hour by hour, digging trenches to juniper trees. The weak and half-frozen sheep followed the shepherds to browse on the greens cut from the trees.

The Navajos met Cold Woman as they met the Hunger People—with calm and fortitude. In his hogan, smoking the tobacco Mr. Hubbell brought, Na Nai sat by the fire, wrapped in a Pendleton blanket. He was in a contemplative mood. He spoke of the snow, saying it was a promise of grass for the sheep, a promise of water in the springtime. Said he:

"I have lived long enough to know that snow comes and snow goes, that sky months follow earth months; that stars move westward, night by night; that the four winds of heaven never cease; that the seven mountains lift their peaks to the clouds and that the Star of the North never sets. I have watched the Morning Star that journeys with the Sun Bearer. Look to the Morning Star, shama. Remember the song in its heart. Out of the white east it comes. Into the evening twilight it goes."

"I shall remember, grandfather. Now, will you tell me how you felt when the American soldiers took your people away to Fort Sumner?"

The old man's eyes took on a hardness. The dreamy quality left them. He answered abruptly:

"I felt afraid of the guns and the bayonets. I was hungry. I was cold. For four years the corn was destroyed by cutworms. Drouth seared what the worms left."

The old man wrapped the blanket closer about him. His voice softened as he said to Mr. Hubbell:

"My grandson, this is good tobacco; better than any we had in the land of our enemies. Did I ever tell you about the beans the Blue Coats gave to us? They were coffee beans. We did not know. We boiled them, and boiled them. For four days we boiled them. What food did we get? No food from coffee beans. We learned to like the water we boiled them in."

Mr. Hubbell laughed. "You had much to learn, grandfather."

"Much, much to learn. Always there is much to learn. Has shama learned about the younger brother of the bear? She painted his tracks

85

The Navajos met the cold with calm and fortitude

around the bear people, but does she know that he is the porcupine, a greater chief than the bear?"

"Shama wishes to learn from you how to draw the porcupine. She has with her the painting you gave her."

I unrolled the paper, unpacked the watercolors. Old Na Nai approved of what I had done. He took the brush in his hand and drew the porcupine by the white mountain.

"Now it is finished in beauty," he said. "It must receive the pollen."

We said good-by and returned to Winslow, Mr. Hubbell to watch out for starving lambs, the interpreter and I to put our notes into shape. The book progressed. When John Curly's work was done he said:

"Good-by, shama. I go now to learn more stories from the medicine men. We shall sit in the hogan on our sheepskins, glad to have wood to burn, coffee to drink, mutton ribs to roast and bubble-bread browning in the iron pot. I shall tell the young men how you write pretty scenery about our children and how you called me Shi Yazhi, your tenderly growing child. The winter is here. I go."

Pinyon season had arrived. In the Zuni mountains the yield of pine nuts promised unusual wealth. Many families were already camped under the trees when Cold Woman turned the camps into mud, slush and wet wood. Some of the Navajos returned to Winslow, bringing with them what nuts they had gathered. Others stayed on stoically, hoping to leave with their wagons and old Ford trucks loaded with full sacks to sell to the traders. The wife of Many Goats remained in the mountains with her husband and children. They chopped limbs from the trees to build shelters, and gathered wood for their camp.

"Just a day or two more," said the valiant woman, "and then we will go home with enough to trade for flour and blankets for the winter. The little one needs a new shirt and shoes."

Snow began to fall that night. Is the early morning when the Indians awoke, they viewed a world mantled in white. The nuts on the ground were buried beneath six inches of snow.

"We will have to spread our blankets beneath the trees," said the wife of Many Goats, "to catch the nuts that fall."

Two more days of snow and colder weather convinced the men that they should leave with what nuts they had gathered. "We will go to the trading post," they said, "and come back with food for our children." Five more days of bad weather and snow piled up so deep that no firewood could be gathered. The despairing women and children went hungry and cold. In the meantime, the outside world of white people, reading their newspapers while they sat comfortably sipping their morning coffee, glanced casually at the report of four hundred Navajos marooned on high mesa tops in unseasonable snows. I could not sleep for worry over inaction in the matter

Lorenzo Hubbell in his trading post

of rescue parties. Already eleven Navajos including a baby had frozen to death.

"There are plenty of airplanes in the country. They could drop food and blankets," I said to Mr. Hubbell.

"The clouds are too low for that," he answered. "I've been phoning to the agency. The government has considered relief."

Throughout the morning the telephone at the agency was kept busy with reports from Washington. "Spare no expense. Use airplanes if necessary," wired the Commissioner of Indian Affairs.

I, who had felt so desperately helpless as an individual, drew strength from the messages and realized with fervor the power of organization. I knew that government trucks and snowplows were making their way to the nut-pickers. With a National Hunger Army marching to the Capitol; with eight million white people unemployed in these United States, Washington had come to the rescue of the Navajos.

Three days later, while snow lay a foot deep on the desert, and yard-long icicles hung from the eaves of Winslow houses, the Indians began to straggle home. Some came on the backs of their scrawny ponies; others drove dilapidated Fords. Some came home in government trucks. Mr. Hubbell and I watched the trail for the wife of Many Goats and her family. They came afoot, bedraggled, thin and frostbitten. She had killed her two ponies for her family to eat, saving her loved ones from starvation. Confidently, she said to Mr. Hubbell:

"We left five sacks of nuts on the mesa top. We burned our wagon for firewood. We ate our ponies for food, but we gathered five sacks of nuts. Shi Yazhi needs new shoes. I need wool to spin."

I felt my heart beat fast and faster as I listened to the tale of heroism. I knew that hundreds of sheep were starving. Sheep which Mr. Hubbell had bought and paid for were unable to reach the grass buried beneath the snow. I knew that the trader could not give the woman what she needed. In that winter of 1931 he had been taxed to the limit of his resources by the low market prices of wool, mutton and pinyons. I knew that he had no flour to sell to the Navajos, for the wholesalers could no longer give credit. My eyes were misty.

When we returned to Winslow in the cold of late afternoon, I said to Mr. Hubbell, "Let us go to the Chinaman's and order two of his fine steaks."

"If we go you will have to pay for the dinner," he answered. "I haven't a cent in my pocket."

This from a successful businessman who in the past could borrow fifty thousand dollars from a local bank with which to buy the sheep of the Navajos. This from a man who had made the practice of traveling from the bank to the trading post with a barrel filled with silver dollars in the back of his car. (Navajos liked to be paid in silver dollars).

The cold spell wrought havoc in my small apartment. Water pipes were frozen and punctured. A spray of icy water reached across the kitchen toward the stove, which I laboriously fed with wood. Inefficiently coping with the situation, I admired to the utmost the wife of Many Goats who could chop up her wagon for firewood, slay her ponies for food, and come smiling through, turning her thoughts to song. I, with a roof over my head, could not keep warm. It became necessary to move to a modest hotel. There, steam heat battled with the freezing temperature. I looked out of the window onto a dull sky, against whose sodden gray one bare-limbed cottonwood reared its delicate branchlets amid tin chimney pots. Scattering snowflakes fell to the street, powdering the tops of automobiles with white. Old quilts tied about radiators bore evidence of the cold.

With weary acceptance of the ugliness, I turned from the window as the landlady entered the room with my mail. Among the letters was one from the publishers telling me that my book, *Waterless Mountain,* had been awarded the Newbery Medal, and that I was expected to travel to New Orleans in April to receive it. Two months were mine before I left, for study, for listening in my own head.

CHAPTER TEN

The Morning Star

ORAIBI BOUND, I arrived at the Hopi village in time to witness a bean dance in an underground kiva. On the morning before that performance I arose at dawn that I might see the Katchina hand out the sprouted beans grown and forced in the kiva. These were given to the children of the village along with Katchina dolls and toy bows and arrows. The day dawned still and calm, disclosing bashful little children standing in doorways waiting for the presents. The older ones tagged along after the bearer of gifts, reminding me of the children following the Pied Piper, only this man carried a rattle. It was dramatic and impressive, a sort of Hopi Santa Claus celebration.

At night I went down the ladder into the crowded kiva. A central stove gave forth heat. I found a seat and watched the young men descend dressed in colorful costumes. They wore enormous conventionalized cowhead masks. There ensued considerable mooing before the whole herd commenced the song and dance. Absorption in the ceremony brought assurance that the mooing and singing would

Hopi Indian village

materialize plentiful food. Presto! The masked dancers produced
steamed corn on the cob and strings of red apples which were dis-
tributed to the audience. All ate apples and threw the cores on the
floor near the stove. The attendant swept them up with a native grass
brush to get ready for the next group of dancers.

Thus was spring brought to Oraibi with the first ceremonial of the
year. On the hill little weeds grew jade-green leaves that hugged the
ground like gem stones. The Hopi children asked me to draw with
them, so I went to school five days a week as I had done on previous
visits to Oraibi. I gathered the day's work and returned to my room
to mount the precious paintings on gray paper. I intended to take
them East with me. Seeking material for the new book kept me
busy. Lorenzo Hubbell, Jr., the trader, helped in every way. Once,
when my mind seemed empty and blank, he said:

"This is a bright, sunny morning with no wind. Take your paper
and pencil and a lunch. Have one of the Hopi boys drive you up to

the top of the mesa. Just sit and wait for something to happen. I'll send the boy back for you at three o'clock."

So I went to a place suspended between heaven and earth, where the air was clean and pure, the sparse shrubbery pungent with health-giving incense. It was so quiet and the distant mountains so far away, I let myself rest. I did not think. I sat in the sunshine alone in far reaches of desert. How blue were the distant hills! How imperceptibly they became blue. From my feet resting on pink gravel, the desert stretched away pink and soft gray-green, and then it was blue with a blue sky above it. The blueness was vibrant witih vitality descending and ascending from sky and earth. Time was no longer. I shut my eyes. My ears heard no sound, but somewhere, somehow in the shell of me I knew that heaven and earth and I were one. I walked in the middle.

Sitting on the high mesa with the glory of sunshine enfolding the desert, I heard someone walking toward me. A very old Hopi from Hotevilla stood beside me. Short, brown and wrinkled, his gray hair hanging about his face, he seeemed like some gnome of the rocks, some genie from the *Arabian Nights'* tales. I wondered if he would present me with a lamp to rub. He leaned down, touched my white dress, felt of my shoes, loooked into my face with a puzzled expression which seemed to say, "Is this a human or what?" Then he spoke the only Hopi word I knew, "Lolami." That word means beautiful. I stood up and waved my hand toward the western mountain, snow-capped; toward Navajo Mountain in the north; toward the whole encompassing horizon where earth melted into sky and I said, "Lolami."

The genie had given me a lamp to rub. It was the word beauty. He walked toward Hotevilla. I began to write of the Navajo idea of the cosmos. The old medicine man, Na Nai, had told me of the four sides of the world, where men of turquoise, white shell, abalone and jet sparkle in their strength, upholding the heavens above; twelve men at every point; north, south, east and west, holding the sky in place. He had told me of the sacred mountains and he said to remember the song in the heart of the Morning Star. I had not been sure about that song. Na Nai took it for granted that I knew it. Why was I making sand paintings if I knew not the songs which went with them? I remembered a day when I visited Na Nai in his hogan and found him in earnest conversation with the learned Snake priest of the Hopis. They were sharing their wisdom. On the floor of the hogan Na Nai outlined with his finger a figure of a four-pointed star. The Snake priest watched, nodded approval. I could not understand their words, but I knew that Sontso, the Morning Star, was under discussion.

On the mesa top, just sitting and waiting for something to happen, knowledge came to me. Before me rose myriad turquoise-tinted dreams of the desert; white-shell dreams, rainbow-hued dreams of abalone; jewels polished by generations of poets seeking the same assurance as white men seek: constancy and peace. The tinted dreams became personified. They were dancers from the four quarters of heaven and earth, those dancers who played their parts in the hundred sand paintings I had copied. When they do not dance in lines of four, they move around a circle, always going sunwise. The circle is the deep center.

I remember a painting from the Big Star Chant where a black star is the center. It is four-pointed, outlined with white rays of light. It serves as the fire in the house of the stars. The star people in the four quarters are of the four colors, dressed in armor, similar to that of the warrior gods, in the Upward-moving Chant. Each has a bow and arrow. From the arms hang long strings with arrow points attached. The headdresses are made of five arrow points. I knew that Sontso represents Venus, the Morning Star. There came to my mind the song of Nayenezgani, child of the Sun-Bearer, slayer of the monsters, saviour of the people of the earth:

The slayer of the Alien Gods,
That now am I.
The Bearer of the Sun

94

THE MORNING STAR

Arises with me.
Goes down with me;
But sees me not.

Then I knew that the beautiful Toltec story of Quetzalcoatl, the Feathered Serpent, white god of the air, saintly ruler and civilizer, had reached the Hopis and the Navajos. Mexican legend tells how Quetzalcoatl taught men to follow his austere and virtuous life, to hate all violence and war, to sacrifice no men nor beasts, but to make mild offerings of bread and flowers. He taught picture writing and the calendar, also the artistic work of the silversmith.

Native tradition holds that when Quetzalcoatl was driven from his kingdom by the artifices of a magician, he journeyed to the seacoast, donned the feather ornament and the mask of turquoise mosaic, as the dead were arrayed on the funeral pile, and cremated himself. The heart flew up to heaven and transformed itself into the Morning Star. This story, so full of the hope of a tortured people, has filtered into the legends of the tribes in the North. It suited the minds of the Navajos weary of war. It suited the Hopis who call themselves the Peaceful People. It became the song in the heart of the Morning Star. It was Lolami.

So absorbed had I become with the legends of the great land, which knows no boundaries in thought, that I was a bit dazed when the automobile came to take me back to Oraibi. I had been traveling on rainbows, on clouds and rafts of sunbeams. I was filled with great joy and wonder when I arrived at the trading post. Mr. Hubbell noticed my exuberance and asked me to tell him what had happened. I described the old Hopi who had touched my garments and said, Lolami. I confessed that I had felt a certain fear that he might become too curious, too intimate. Mr. Hubbell said:

"No. It was only that you are so white, that he said Lolami. Besides, you are wearing the turquoise."

As I look back upon my Navajo-Hopi experiences I think that the two months spent working on my book in Oraibi held more peace

An old Hopi man, an old kiva, an old belief

than any two months of my life. Fine old medicine men spent hours telling me of their legends. Mr. Hubbell translated with rare understanding. When it came time for me to leave for the railroad, he took from his safe necklaces of silver and turquoise, bracelets of rare design, rings set with blue-sky stones.

"Show them to the people you meet, wear what you care to, sell any you can," he said. "Keep the turquoise near you, then you will not forget us here on the desert."

I was wearing on my finger the blue piece I had found in the sand that Thanksgiving Day years before. It was set in old silver made by some long-haired silversmith working beneath a turquoise sky. I would not forget, nor would there be erased from my memory a sand storm which raged for four days before I left. It blew dust under the dooors, in every crevice of the house, piled it up on the porch. It obscured the disk of the sun, turning it and the dim rays it sent to turquoise blue. It stood looking out upon the desert world and I marveled that the orb itself had become a turquoise pendant in the deep above.

CHAPTER ELEVEN

Twelve White Plumes

CHRISTMAS EVE found me alone in my eight-sided house. When blackness settled upon the outside world, I placed two red candles in the south window. I lit them. Their feeble rays flickered in an infinitude of wilderness. They were dedicated to my husband and son, thousands of miles away in the East. The night was still, voiceless, aphonic. Peace settled upon me as I lay upon the bed, with no inclination to sleep. An hour passed. The candles burned low. I snuffed out the flame.

As if the extinction of light were a signal, there arose in the hush of midnight, the sound of Navajo voices—men's voices singing in chorus. The manifestation was overpowering as the howling, wild notes filled the air. The rhythm became hypnotic. It was rhythm born of the wind on the mesas, of rain on the cornfields, of the yelping of coyotes. At times, falsetto notes, incredibly high, told that some goddess was impersonated. Again, staccato notes, sharp and monotonous signified the approach of the war gods. The farm songs of Haste-hogan, the house god, told of the vigil of the corn, the weeding of the corn and its harvesting.

I opened my bedroom door and looked down upon the chanters grouped about the small hogan at the foot of the knoll. There must have been thirty young Navajos singing in ecstasy, filled with joy over the return of the sun. Far up on a shoulder of Waterless Mountain there burned a huge bonfire. Had it been lit as a new fire ritual? I believe so. I felt the ancientness of man's joy in the winter solstice. I was glad to be alone with Waterless Mountain, its hopeful fire, its serenading young men. All night long they sang. When dawn came and with it the trader's family, I arose to begin the day's activities. I knew that for me this was a farewell to Navajo Land. All day the people arrived to receive gifts prepared for them. They were an orderly, happy lot, wearing their warm winter coats, fleece-lined, their Pendleton robes and full skirts. Several madonnas of the desert brought their babes tied to cradle boards.

Shi Yazhi stood beneath the Christmas wreath of juniper and fir which hung upon the screen door of the porch. The wreath was minus a fine red-satin bow which had proved too tempting and too easily procurable for some color-hungry Indian. Shi Yazhi wore the emerald-green kerchief tied around his forehead. He was surely singing in his heart that Christmas morning, for a smile brightened his face as his hand clasped a newly acquired pocketknife sent from New York.

When evening came, the candles on the tree were lit for the few white guests, who spontaneously sang "Holy Night." All of us, brown and white, were united in the strong bond of children of the sun. Down through the ages the brothers and sisters had struggled to survive. In my lotus-flower house of eight walls which I was to leave forever on the morrow, I could feel the blesssing which had descended upon us. The fire on Waterless Mountain no longer burned, but the Yule log of my English ancestors glowed upon the hearth.

The fire of desert comradeship still burns in my consciousness. It lights the trail of my mind as it travels to the Old Age River lined with castles of a forgotten people. My mind turns to Quetzalcoatl, great craftsman, great teacher of the American continent, made god-

My house on the hill

like in legends which passed into the stories of later tribes. As god of the dawn, Quetzalcoatl became for the Navajos one of their lesser deities, Hasteyalti, dwelling in the House of Dawn and Evening Twilight. He wears the twelve white plumes as a headdress and is always ready to succor the needy.

When I found the song of "This I Walk With," in Washington Matthews monumental work, *The Night Chant, a Navajo Ceremonial,* I felt that I was listening to Lao-Tzu, the sage who knew the Way, the simplicity of spontaneity, action without motive, free from all selfish purpose. Thinking of the venerable Chinese sage, my thoughts leaped to old Na Nai, singer of the Mountain Chant. If any individual ever "Conducted affairs without feeling the trouble of them, who accounted the great small and the small as great, and recompensed injury with kindness," it was Na Nai who crawled over the desert sand for sixty years to sing and to heal his people. I place the first white plume in the crown I am making, in the name of Na Nai. There follows the eagle feather of Ashi, the shaman who made on the floor of the schoolroom at Oraibi a sand painting, sharing his knowledge with the Hard-working Woman.

Moquitso, virtuoso in the fine art of pouring sand, whose capacious memory drew from the depths of his learning, a hundred sand-painting designs, was most outstanding in his statement that evil must not be portrayed. He gave to me the paintings with their meanings taken from chants which are fast becoming extinct. To him, ethnologists owe a debt of gratitude.

For my own particular satisfaction, I place a plume for Big Mustache, singer of the Coyote Chant. His philosophy upheld me with the words: "He who creates beauty never tires."

As I write, there moves in and out of my mind the small boy in Blue Canyon, herding his mother's sheep among fantastic sandstone cliffs, where her rocks vie with white in weird conglomeration. He sang the songs his uncle taught him and he made songs of his own when his friends—the eagles, the winds, the soft rain and yellow Mariposa lilies—told him the essence of their being. For his songs he was honored with a turquoise bead to tie in his black hair. His plume joins the others in this coronet of white feathers edged with red rays of the sun.

Henry, searching for ta-da-teen, the pollen which means peace and righteousness to deep-feeling desert men, has his plume for the eagerness of his search and for his words to me, "If my mother says that I will get ta-da-teen, I will." Henry knew that to reach his goal, he must identify himself with the law of the universe, and reach that point where he could say, "It is I, I walk with."

The seventh feather is for Hasteen Sani, an aristocrat in feature and carriage despite the fact that his Levis were patched at the knees with flour sacks. He was scrupulously clean, washed his clothes himself and sewed the famous patches on his pants. Hasteen Sani wore the badge of poverty in a royal manner. When he placed a section of my yo-yo quilt about his waist, he had visions of himself as a youth dancing all night until Doli, the bluebird, sang of the dawn. Hasteen Sani loved us. He conferred the greatest honor upon us by saying that we were Navajos.

Klitso, the carpenter who built my eight-sided house, has already had a feather placed in his cap by no less an admirer than Theodore Roosevelt, who wrote an article for *The Outlook* of October 18, 1913. The President of the United States visited Arizona and witnessed the Snake Dance at Walpi in August 1913. He wrote:

No white visitor to Walpi was quite as interesting as an Indian visitor, a Navajo Indian who was the owner and chauffeur of the motor in which Mr. Hubbell had driven to Walpi. He was an excellent example of the Indian who ought to be given a chance to go to a non-reservation school—a class not perhaps as yet relatively large but growing steadily larger. He had gone to such a school; and at the close of his course had entered the machine shops of the Santa Fe and Northeastern Railway—I think that was the name of the road—staying there four years, joining the local union, going out with the other men when they struck, and

Navajo friends at my eight-sided house

Moquitso, the Navajo medicine man, who gave me nearly a hundred sand paintings—now in the University of California, Berkeley, and Arizona State University, Tucson

having in all ways precisely the experience of an average skilled mechanic. Then he returned to the reservation, where he is now a prosperous merchant, running two stores, and he purchased his automobile as a matter of convenience and economy of time, so as to get quickly from one store to the other, as they are far apart. He is not a Christian nor is his wife; but his children have been baptized in the Catholic Church. Of course such a prosperous career is exceptional for an Indian as it would be for a white man; but there were Hopi Indians whom we met at the dance, both storekeepers and farmers, whose success had been almost as great.

If Theodore Roosevelt could have watched Klitso plying his trade as he constructed the octagonal house at Black Mountain, I think he would have been as thrilled as I. Klitso still observed an eight-hour day. He carried no watch but measured time by the sun. He constructed a simple sun dial. When a shadow fell in a certain place he told his helpers it was time to eat the noonday meal. As foreman, Klitso received five dollars a day for his excellent craftsmanship. His helpers were paid two dollars. He designed a front door made of mill slabs. It was accomplished entirely by hand, perfect in design. When it came to making a chimney, Klitso told me he had taken a correspondence course in chimney building. He could understand the construction details, but please would I be so kind as to do the arithmetic for him. I must find the square of the opening of the hearth, divide it by ten, then he would know what the area for the opening of the top of the chimney should be. I did the arithmetic and was awestruck as Klitso proceeded to build. The result was a perfectly good draught with no smoke in the room. A deluxe mantelshelf evolved out of one long sandstone slab. Klitso was in his element as a craftsman. I think Quetzalcoatl would have approved of him and I know that Theodore Roosevelt would have been as delighted as I.

Loud Talker won his place as a white plume. On the morning

Laura Adams Armer and Sidney Armer in their garden
at Fortuna, California

after Christmas he helped pack the precious vegetable-dye rugs and the priceless copies of sand paintings. There came with him, certain small children bearing gifts of arrowheads, fossilized sharks' teeth, toe joints of some huge reptilian monster, imprints in sandstone of ammonites, those very ancient coiled denizens of a salt sea. The past eons of Mother Earth's life were represented in the slender hands of the brown-eyed children. These gentle ones I had not seen before. They came from faraway hogans. They were natural, unspoiled children who miraculously had escaped the contamination of greedy self-seekers. They spoke no word to me; just held out their delicate brown hands disclosing the gifts which Mother Earth had fashioned into forms and designs too mysterious for comprehension. The ammonite impressions spiraled both sunwise and counterclockwise. One little hand held a pottery sherd with a spiral design matching the ammonite inprint.

The crown of twelve white plumes is completed by the three children, names unknown, who brought their treasures found eight thousand feet above sea level; treasures of the ocean which once covered the area where the Old Age River winds its way to the Colorado.